the BIG
FARM BOOK

the BIG FARM BOOK

By Annie Ingle

Illustrations by Aurelius Battaglia

Platt & Munk, Publishers / New York

"Cockadoodledoo!"

"Rise and shine!" Father Baxter calls out cheerily, just in case some Baxters didn't hear the rooster.

It is 4:30 in the morning. Four-thirty is practically the middle of the night for city people. Most of them are fast asleep. But for farm folk like the Baxters, it is first thing in the morning and time to get up.

Mother Baxter and Father Baxter have been up already for an hour. They've been busy . . .

   lacing on their boots,
   chopping wood for the wood-burning stove,
   slicing bacon into nice, thick strips.

Now the aroma of bacon frying on the griddle travels upstairs and daughter Josie and son Jamie and Grammy and Grandpa hurry and put on their clothes. It is breakfast time—the best time of all.

There is hardly a scrap of conversation at the breakfast table, for look at all there is to eat. Not just eggs and bacon. There are eggs and bacon *and* hotcakes and butter and maple syrup and sausage. There are blueberry muffins, still steaming from the oven. There are homefries and grits and pitchers of fresh fruit juice and milk, steaming mugs of hot coffee and tea and cocoa.

Breakfast on a farm is by far the most important meal of the day. Breakfast anywhere is important, but on a farm, even though there are plenty of machines to help, there are chores to be done from dawn until dusk.

10

"You can't plow and plant on an empty stomach!" Father Baxter declares, as he helps himself to another blueberry muffin.
While Father and Josie tidy up the kitchen, Grammy and Jamie are off to the chicken coop to collect eggs, and to feed and water the poultry stock.

The Baxter farm has dozens of chickens, but it isn't a poultry farm. It has pigs and cows, too, but it isn't a piggery or a dairy. The Baxter's is a family farm. A family farm raises small amounts of many different products. Some products, like strawberries and pumpkins, the Baxters take to market. Other products, like tomatoes and chickens, the Baxters raise just for family use. A big industrial farm, like the egg farm across the road, raises vast amounts of just one product and sells it all. On the egg farm, hundreds of hens lay thousands of eggs onto a conveyor belt. Machines then screen, clean, and plop eggs into containers.

Grammy has always lived on a family farm and she would not have it any other way. But family farms have changed quite a bit since she was a girl. She remembers when there was no such thing as chicken wire. Chicken yards weren't fenced in. The hens made their nests off in the bushes. You had to hunt for the eggs and find them before they spoiled. It was great fun, but it sometimes took all morning to complete just that one chore.

Looking after the pigs is Josie's favorite chore. Whenever they hear people coming, the pigs scoot out of sight into the pig house. But the pigs are used to Josie so they venture out to greet her. Josie knows each of the pigs by name. Penny, the piglet, is her special favorite.

Every day, Josie cleans and scours the cement floor of the pig house and makes sure they are pleased with the slops.

Mother Baxter dumps fresh slops into the troughs. Slops is made of ears of corn and scraps from the table.

Contrary to popular opinion, pigs are very neat eaters. On hot summer days, they cool their delicate pink skins with cool, clean mud. Otherwise, they prefer to pass their time in nice, tidy pens.

Time for the morning milking.

Cows are hardly ever milked by hand. Nowadays, machines make fast work of milking. First, the udders of the cows are sponged clean. Then the suction cups of the milkers are attached. The cows are all milked at once. The milk from each cow runs into one large tank. Each cow gives 40 pounds of milk a day. The cows are used to being hooked up to the milker twice a day. They

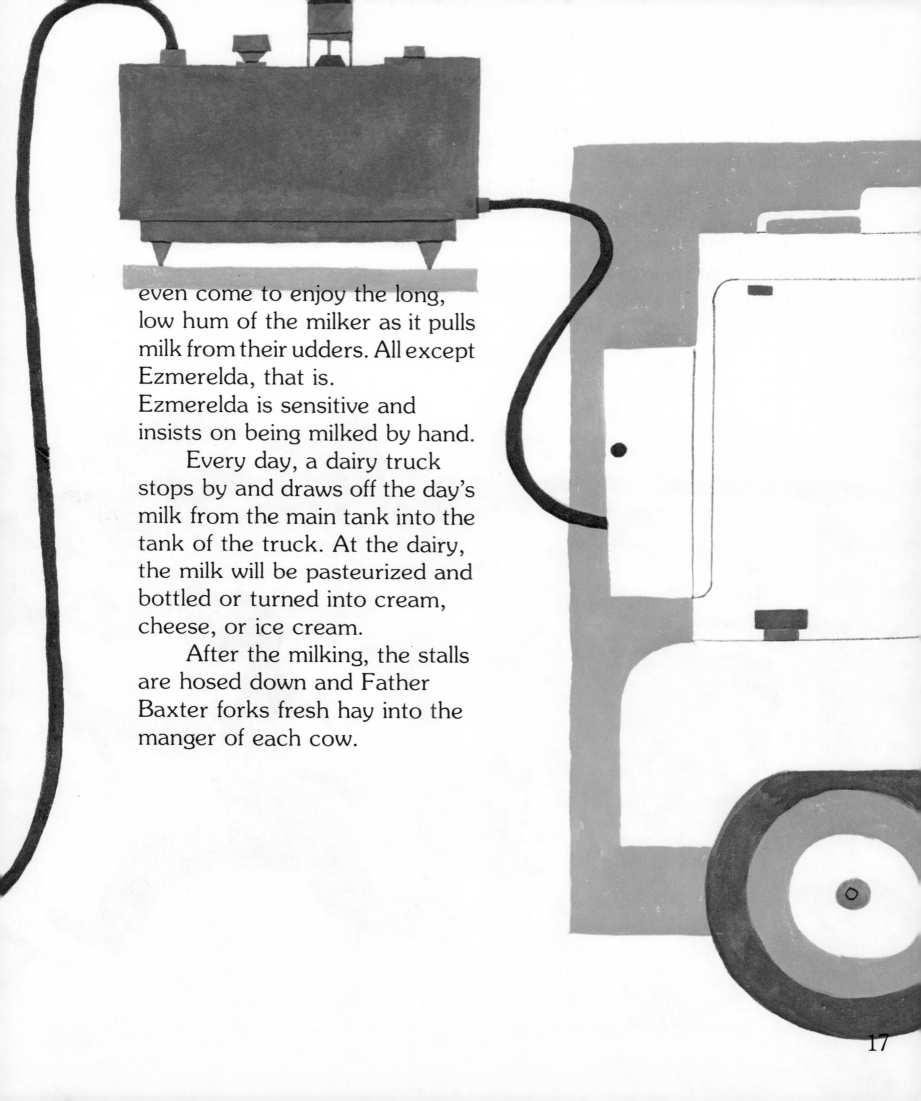

even come to enjoy the long, low hum of the milker as it pulls milk from their udders. All except Ezmerelda, that is. Ezmerelda is sensitive and insists on being milked by hand.

Every day, a dairy truck stops by and draws off the day's milk from the main tank into the tank of the truck. At the dairy, the milk will be pasteurized and bottled or turned into cream, cheese, or ice cream.

After the milking, the stalls are hosed down and Father Baxter forks fresh hay into the manger of each cow.

Whenever the weather is mild, the cows go out to pasture soon after the morning milking. So that the cows can graze in peace, the Baxters have set aside a few acres too rocky and too marshy for plowing. Josie and Old Boo, the family dog, drive the cows out to pasture. Boo makes sure no one of the cows loses her way or heads for the orchards.

In the pasture, there are plenty of shade trees to stand beneath and clover and grass to graze on. Later, Josie will bring out Brian and Belinda, the two horses.

Josie makes sure to close the pasture gate behind them. Once, she forgot and left it ajar. It took the Baxters and their neighbors until well past midnight to round up all the strayed cows. All except Ezmerelda. Timid Ezmerelda never left the pasture.

This year's corn crop has to be put in. The Baxters grow corn for animal feed, and for people food, too. The field the Baxters are planting corn in this year, was left bare, or fallow, last year, so that the soil could regain some of its richness. Each crop takes nutriments from the soil. If the same crop were to be planted in the same plot, year after year, it would not be long before the field grew barren and the crop weak. Sometimes, instead of leaving the field empty, a crop of clover is planted and then plowed under come plowing time.

Plowing is the first step in planting. Pulling the plow attachment behind the tractor, Father Baxter turns up the soil to make a bed for the seeds. The plow attachment has discs which chop up the soil as they rotate behind the moving tractor. The plow cuts eight lines, or furrows, at a time.

Now that the furrows are dug, the earth is ready to receive the corn seeds.

Driving right behind Father's plow, Grandpa uses a tractor attachment that does two jobs, one right after another. First, a vibrating box scatters the corn seeds. As the tractor rumbles up and down the furrows, the seed boxes jiggle and vibrate and shake eight

rows of corn seeds that fall neatly in the eight furrows. Then, the second part of the attachment, another plow, follows the seed shaker and turns the soil back under, along with the newly dropped seeds.

No, that's not a hired hand, that's Boo, along for the ride.

In spite of modern farming methods, some plants just cannot be planted by machines. If you took the seeds of the strawberry and sprinkled them by planter attachment and covered them by plow attachment and let nature take its course, not much would happen. Plants such as strawberries and tomatoes need tender loving care to be started on their growth. That is why there are plant nurseries.

Mother Baxter has a strawberry and tomato nursery. Each is located on the back of an old flatbed truck. She covers the

truck bed with plastic to create a sort of greenhouse on wheels. She watches over the plants carefully, watering and fertilizing, and pruning and spraying each individual plant until they are big enough and healthy enough to fend for themselves out in the fields. Then she drives the flatbed into a newly plowed field and transplants each plant by hand. The rest of the family helps, but it is hard, back-aching work. It is less back-aching, the family has found, if they think of strawberries and cream, strawberry shortcake and strawberry tarts as they work.

Summer is here
and with it, the
usual long, dry spells.
The same well
that supplies the house
and the barn with water,
also supplies
the irrigation water
for the
crops.

26

The well pump is powered by the wind. When the wind moves the sails of the windmill, the pump motor runs, bringing up fresh, clear water from the spring hidden deep in the earth, and keeps the water tank full. During dry spells such as this, the Baxters run pipes along the rows of crops. Just as people in the suburbs water their lawns with a sprinkler, the Baxters water their crops with an irrigation system. This system keeps the parched plants moist until the next rain falls.

Yearly pest control is an important part of farming. Among the things the pilgrims brought over with them from Europe were some 100,000 species of insects that are harmful to crops, animals, and trees. Each crop has its own arch enemy.

Scientists have come up with chemicals that control these enemies. The Baxters have a farm large enough that it needs a plane to spray the chemicals. But the farm is not so large that they need to keep a plane of their own. Each year, they hire a flyer whose job it is to spray crops.

On a dry, windless day, the crop sprayer comes. The Baxters have marked each row of crops with a different colored marker so that the sprayer can tell which rows he has sprayed already and which he has yet to spray. Back and forth, back and forth, up the green row, down the red row, the flyer swoops low, spraying the crops with protective chemicals.

The chemicals are strong enough that the rain won't wash them off. That is why it is important to wash vigorously whatever fruits and vegetables you buy in the market before you cook or eat them.

It is the middle of summer. The crops are in, the daily chores are done. Everybody heads for the shade and a tall, cool drink. Everybody, that is, but Father. Father has a project in mind. Before

long, he has everybody pitching in. After years of talking about it, they finally are going to dig that swimming hole.

In the pasture is a swampy, muddy pond. With a neighbor's bulldozer, they scoop it out wide and deep and even. They line it with tar paper and a truckload of fine, white sand.

With rain barrels and some broad planks, they build a float.

Father dumps in a few big trout from the local fish hatchery.

From now on, on hot summer days such as this, the Baxters won't have to drive all the way into town to the public swimming pool. They have their own pool. The Baxters and their friends waste no time trying it out.

It may take a few summers for the cows to get used to all the splashing and commotion in the middle of their once peaceful pasture.

The haying is the hardest of all summer jobs.

Because it is the main winter feed of farm animals, hay is still one of the most important crops on the Baxter's and any other farm where it will grow.

When Grandpa was a boy, he cut hay with a scythe and raked it into bundles called windrows. He heaved the windrows onto a haywagon. It took days to harvest a single hay crop. It was a most worrisome time because the hay had to be cut and stored before it rained. Wet hay is useless hay.

Nowadays, the mechanical hayloader and baler make the haying less difficult and worrisome. The mechanical loader and baler cuts the hay and bundles it into tight bales. But even modern weather experts can be fooled by a surprise cloudburst. So come haying time, all the Baxters and some hired hands work round the clock. They work in shifts, through the night under high-powered spotlights, until the acres of hay have been baled and stored away safely and dryly in the hayloft of the barn.

Now that the hardest job of the summer is done, the whole family feels that it deserves a good time.

While everybody waits in line
to shower off the last of the hayseeds and dust,
Father hitches up
Brian and Belinda
to the old wagon
and piles on a few bales of hay.

34.

Everybody has put on nice, clean clothes. Jamie tunes up his ukelele. The whole family piles onto the haywagon. They're off into the warm summer night.

It's a hayride! Old-fashioned, perhaps, but still the finest summer fun on the farm.

But where are they off to on this hayride?

To a square dance! Where else?

It's square dance night.

The Baxter's neighbors have cleared out their barn and hung crepe paper and balloons from the rafters. People from all the nearby farms have come to dance. The travelling square dance band and the caller have already set up for the first round.

Everybody—even the kids—dances to the square dance caller's instructions. You don't have to know the steps, just listen to the call:

"Lead to the left. Lead to the right. Swing your partner and hold her tight. Allemand, left, and Doh-See-Doh. Then go round to the start and bow real low."

The kitchen garden is Mother Baxter's pride and joy. It is the product of several generations of proud gardeners. All summer long, it has yielded up fresh peas and asparagus, fine tender heads of lettuce and cabbage. Most of the kitchen garden crop is for the Baxter table, while some is for roadstands and for neighbors.

Mother works in the kitchen garden every day. Every day, rain or shine, she is out there, inspecting and weeding, planting and picking.

The flower garden is more beautiful than ever. Grammy snips some petunias for the supper table centerpiece. According to Grammy, no family table should be without its centerpiece of fresh-cut or dried flowers.

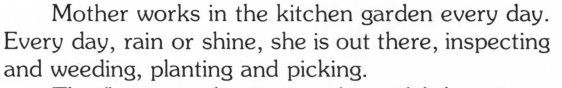

The apples and the peaches
are ripe and ready to be picked.
There is no machine to help, so
the Baxters and some hired helpers
pitch in to pick. Make sure that step-
ladder is secure! The grown-ups use
stepladders but Jamie and Josie prefer
shimmying up the trunks. Watch you
don't shake those branches, Jamie! A
bruised apple or peach will be turned
down by the buyers. After the crop has
been carefully packed in bushel
baskets, the bushels are trucked off to
local roadside stands.

It's a fine old orchard, famous for its delicious Delicious apples. "We try for quality, not quantity," boast Grandpa and Father, both.

The apple orchard was planted by Grandpa's father, with seeds he brought with him from his native England.

Every year, for a solid week, Mother disappears into the pantry to put up preserves. She stops all her other chores. She even stops doing her share of the cooking.

Preserving foods means putting them in airtight containers — like mason jars — so that they can be kept without refrigeration for long periods of time. All winter long, when there are no fresh vegetables and fruits to eat, Mother's preserves give the family the vitamins they need to stay healthy.

To put up strawberry preserves, she steams the strawberries in corn syrup. Then she ladles the fruit into sterilized jars and pours on a layer of parafin, or wax, which hardens and seals in the food product.

Some vegetables—like asparagus and peas and carrots—she cooks, just a little, and then freezes in plastic containers in the long, deep freeze. Mother Baxter's pantry has row upon row of jars of preserves, each carefully labeled as to contents and the date of jarring.

Even more delicious than preserved fruit is fresh fruit pie. Grammy makes just about the most delicious cherry pie anyone has ever tasted. The children can scarcely wait until it has cooled on the windowsill to get their slices.

School is open again.

Jamie and Josie don't really mind. It has been a long and busy summer. They haven't seen most of their good friends since last term. And now, they don't have to get up quite so early. Father lets them sleep until almost six o'clock. At 8:00 A.M. sharp, they must be out in front of the house by the mailbox where the yellow school bus picks them up. The bus drops them off at their front door at 4:00 P.M. Door to door service!

Both Jamie and Josie belong to the 4-H Club, just as their parents did when they were children. The 4-H Club is to country children what Girl and Boy Scouts is to city children. The four h's stand for head, heart, hands and health. The 4-H Club teaches children how to be the best country citizens possible. It teaches them animal husbandry, which is the care, feeding and breeding of farm animals. It teaches them the newest planting methods. It teaches them sewing and cooking and farm management.

This year, Josie is raising a heifer for her special 4-H Club project. Jamie is experimenting with tomatoes and new types of fertilizer. They plan to enter their projects in the county fair, which opens tomorrow.

Jamie and Josie are not the only Baxters entering projects in the County Fair. In fact, each of the Baxters enters something every year. Mother is entering her prize plum preserves and a batch of sweet pickles. Father is entering a strain of corn he has been breeding for years. Grammy and Grandpa are entering a king-sized quilt. Grammy and Grandpa's quilts have won blue ribbons every year for as long as anyone can remember. They are famous for their quilts.

Everybody loads his or her project into the station wagon. They're off to the County Fair.

There are enough activities at the County Fair to keep Baxters of all ages busy every single second of the three days and nights the fair runs. The County Fair has all the best qualities of a circus, an amusement park, and a Fourth of July picnic.

It's difficult not to look everywhere at once. There are corn-shucking contests and log-rolling contests. There are horse races and three-legged races and tractor races. There are livestock contests and pie-baking contests and pickle contests and chicken contests.

Grammy and Grandpa are flattered, as usual, to receive the blue ribbon for their king-sized quilt.

Father Baxter can't resist trying his hand at the greased pig-catching contest.

No matter how much you love pie, a pie-eating contest can exhaust a person.

After three days, the Baxters are tired but pleased. They have done all there is to do. They have won their ribbons. It's time to return to the farm.

The fun is over until next year. It is time for the final harvest before the frost.

The vegetables must be picked and trucked off to roadside stands. Fields of squash are ripe. A whole field of pumpkins must be picked by hand. Jamie and Josie get the pick of the crop.

It's that creepy, delicious time of year! Pumpkin pie and jack-o-lanterns. Jamie and Josie carve their jack-o-lanterns right in the field. This way there is no need to spread newspaper. And the seeds they spill this year will be big fat pumpkins next year.

The corn must be harvested now, too. The Baxters raise fields of corn for the market, and for their own animal feed, too. At the processing plant, the corn will be turned into corn meal and corn flour. On the farm, it is stored in the silo for feed.

The corn harvester picks the corn from the stalks, pulls the kernels off the cobs and shoots the kernels into sacks.

The sacks
are trucked
to the rail-
road station
where they
will be
weighed and
loaded
aboard grain
trains and
taken off to
the process-
ing plants.
The corn
that is used
for feed is
kept on the
cob and car-
ried up to
the silo by
conveyor
belt.

53

It is winter. It may be brisk outside, but inside, everyone takes life slow and easy. It is time to . . .

catch up on reading,

pore over a puzzle,

stare into the fire,

crochet a shawl.

Winter chores are mostly all indoor chores. Most of the animals stay in their houses. Those houses must be kept clean and warm.

Machinery needs mending and upkeep. Blades need to be sharpened, parts oiled, outsides painted with rust-proof paint.

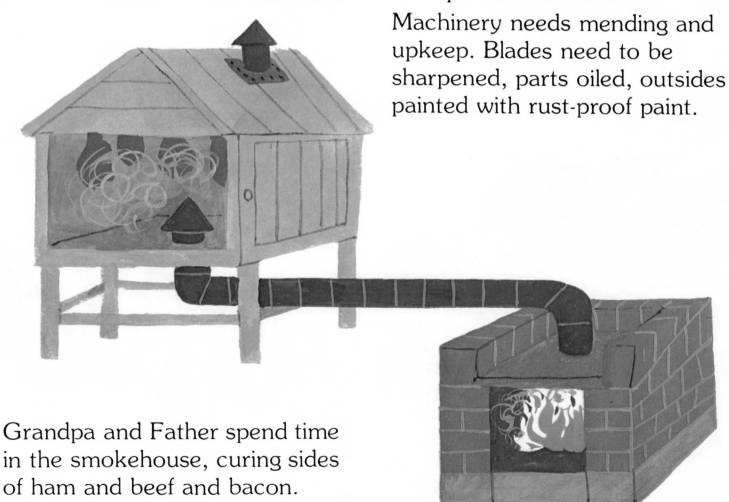

Grandpa and Father spend time in the smokehouse, curing sides of ham and beef and bacon.

Outdoors, most activities are just plain fun. Brian and Belinda get their exercise hooked up to Grandpa's old sleigh. The reins have genuine sleighbells that jingle merrily in the winter air. The swimming hole now comes in handy as a skating pond. And, since Father has stocked it with prime trout, Jamie can do a little winter ice fishing.

Some days the snow is so deep, you need snowshoes just to get to the barn.

Some days, it is so warm the barnyard is as muddy as a pig pen. (Not the Baxter pig pen, of course.)

More and more, nowadays, the barnyard is muddy. Could it be that spring is near?

57

Spring is a time to be born.

There are tiny green buds on all the trees. Up through the mud sprouts new grass. The clover is out.

Something else is happening, too.

Babies.

Everywhere the Baxters look, it seems, there are babies being born and babies following in line behind their mothers. Sometimes the veterinarian comes to help. Sometimes Grammy and Mother help. Most times, animals help themselves. And sometimes, if you're lucky and there at the right time, you can watch.

baby pigs: piglets

baby cats: kittens

baby ducks: ducklings

baby horses: colts

baby chickens: chicks

And high up in the eaves of the barn, there are even baby owls: owlets.

baby cows: calves

Spring isn't only a time for cuddling little babies and smelling the new flowers. Spring is a time for much hard work. For a start, there is spring cleaning. The winter was a rough one and heavy snow and sleet damaged fences and over-weighted roofs. Broken fences and sagging roofs must be mended. The orchard must be inspected for damage. Broken branches must be properly pruned.

Luckily for the Baxters, no great damage was done. But the neighbors were less fortunate. The neighbors lost a barn. What happens when a country neighbor loses a barn, is a barn-raising.

Barn-raising is
a tradition which dates
back to the days of the pioneers.
The pioneers helped each other harvest
and build and, in the event of loss or damage, rebuild.
The family needing the new barn supplies the building materials.
The neighbors supply the muscle and the ingenuity . . . and good food
and gossip about what has been happening all winter long.

It has been a long, hard busy day. Spirits and appetites are high. Mother Baxter and Jamie have left the barn-raising early to make supper. And what a supper it is!

The Baxter table is full to bursting with family and friends and good food. It's feast time.

Friends have all gone home. It is a quiet, peaceful time around the fire. Each Baxter is lost in his or her own thoughts of the past year, the year to come. Grammy and Grandpa are underway with a new quilt. Josie and Father are discussing putting in the new corn crop tomorrow. Mother and Jamie pore over a particularly puzzling jig-saw puzzle.

Soon, more and more Baxters begin to yawn.

"Time to hit the sack for me!" says Father, rising and stretching. One by one, the Baxters are off to bed. One by one, the house lights go out. Soon, the whole house is hushed: the whole family is asleep in a deep, satisfied, exhausted sleep.

The End